SHEEP

A TRUE BOOK

by

Sara Swan Miller

Children's Press®
A Division of Grolier Publishing
New York London Hong Kong Sydney
Danbury, Connecticut

Bighorn sheep

Reading Consultant
Linda Cornwell
Coordinator of School Quality
and Professional Improvement
Indiana State Teachers Association

Content Consultant
Jan Jenner

Visit Children's Press® on the Internet at:
http://publishing.grolier.com

Library of Congress Cataloging-in-Publication Data

Miller, Sara Swan.
    Sheep / by Sara Swan Miller.
        p. cm. — (A True book)
    Includes bibliographical references and index.
    Summary: Describes the physical traits, lifestyle, and behavior of sheep
and their role in providing humans with wool and meat.
    ISBN 0-516-21580-9 (lib. bdg.)   0-516-27184-9 (pbk.)
    1. Sheep Juvenile literature. [1. Sheep] I. Title. II. Series
SF375. 2 .M56   2000
636.3—dc21   99-32312
                                                      CIP

Contents

Sheep graze in a pasture in Ireland.

The Sheep Story

Have you ever come across a flock of sheep grazing on a sunny hillside? It's fun to watch the lambs frisking around their mothers!

Shepherds, people who make a living looking after sheep, enjoy watching their sheep, too. But that's not why they raise them. Sheep are raised for their meat and wool. You may even be wearing something made of wool right now. In some places, people use their milk. Have you ever had Romano cheese on your spaghetti? It was made of sheep milk.

People have been keeping sheep for thousands of years. In Iran, someone found a statue of a woolly sheep that was six thousand years old.

This girl is eating lamb for dinner (above).

Roquefort cheese is made from sheep milk (left).

As in ancient times, these shepherds in Morocco watch over a flock of sheep.

People have kept sheep longer than that—maybe as long as ten thousand years.

The first sheep people tamed were wild sheep called mouflons. There are still mouflons living wild today. Over time people bred the best females, or ewes, with the

A Mouflon sheep

best males, or rams. That way they created many different breeds, or types, of sheep. Some breeds give better wool. Some give better meat. Some can stand harsh climates better. Now there are more than two hundred breeds of sheep. Shepherds choose the breed that suits them best.

A Land of Sheep

New Zealand is a small country. It has more sheep than anywhere else in the world, however. There are fewer than 4 million people living there. The number of sheep? 50 million!

Nearly half of the land in New Zealand is given over to raising sheep. The country is famous for its lamb, wool, and cheese and other sheep milk products. They are sold all over the world.

Workers show off a sheep's fleece.

A wheel of sheep cheese.

A Southdown sheep

Some Favorite Breeds

Merino sheep are raised for their fine wool. They are hardy and can live a long time.

Southdowns are raised for their meat. Because they're small, they're good for small farms.

A Dall sheep

Dall sheep live in Alaska
and parts of Canada. Their
wool is pure white.

A Churro sheep

Churro sheep have amazing horns. They live in New Mexico.

15

Romney sheep

Romneys come from a place where it is very rainy and windy. They can survive in harsh weather that other breeds can't stand.

Cheviots are bred to take care of themselves, and they are very hardy. Cheviot wool is very strong and long-lasting.

Friesian (FREE-zhun) Milk Sheep give more milk than any other breed of sheep. They need more care than other breeds, however.

Sheep farmers round up and sort their flock.

What Are Sheep Like?

Sheep stay together in groups called flocks. This may be because they enjoy each other's company. Also, there's safety in numbers. Sheep are timid animals. They have no sharp teeth or claws to fight with. They can't defend them-selves from coyotes, stray

A coyote chases a sheep.

dogs, or other predators.
Shepherds usually keep their
sheep inside strong fences to
protect them.

Sheep are easy animals to
keep. In the warm summer

This large roll of hay feeds a lot of sheep.

months they eat mostly grass. As long as there is plenty of hay, or mowed and dried grass, for them to eat, and some water, they don't need other food.

Grass is hard to digest, so a sheep has a special stomach. A sheep's stomach has four parts. When a sheep eats a mouthful of grass, it chews it only enough to wet it. Then it goes down into the first two parts of the sheep's stomach. When the sheep is full, it lies down and brings up a wad of grass called cud. It chews it thoroughly this time. Then the cud goes into the last two parts of the sheep's stomach to be digested.

Sheep can live on rocky, hilly pastures where other animals couldn't survive so easily.

A sheep's split hoof

Their sharp split hooves help them climb over rough ground. They need less to eat, too. Flocks of sheep even live in deserts. The shepherds guide them from place to place to find patches of grass.

Many strands of soft wool make up a sheep's fleece.

Sheep have thick wool called fleece. Have you ever stuck your fingers into a sheep's deep, thick fleece? Your hands will get very oily. Sheep have a strong-smelling oil called lanolin in the fleece that helps waterproof it.

People use it to make skin lotion.

Rams are active and ornery. There is usually only one ram in a flock. The ewes are gentle. In the fall, the ram mates with all the ewes. Five months later, the lambs are born. Usually one or two lambs are born at a time. The ewe has only two teats to nurse them. If it has a third lamb, the shepherd usually has to feed it from a bottle.

A ewe nurses its lambs.

The mother licks the new-born clean and calls to it with a special cry, or bleat. The lamb can stand up by itself to nurse soon after it is born.

This lamb is one day old.

When they're not nursing or resting, lambs love to romp and play with each other. They run and leap about, bleating noisily. They nurse from their mother for about five months until they can live on grass alone. Their high bleats slowly turn into a low "baah-baah." They become more interested in eating than in playing. In only six months, they're all grown up.

A Black-faced sheep
and its black lambs

In summer, there is plenty for sheep to eat in the pasture.

Sheep on a Small Farm

During the summer months, sheep don't need much attention. The shepherd checks the flock every day to make sure the sheep are healthy and safe. Some shepherds put the flock in an apple orchard for a while. The sheep keep the grass short.

Hungry sheep at the feeding trough

In the winter, there's more work to do. The shepherd brings the sheep into a shed to protect them. Sheep can survive the cold. They can not survive drafts, however. The shed is usually three-sided. It's open on one side, so the sheep can wander about in the yard on nice days. The shed needs to be big enough for the whole flock. Sheep should not be overcrowded.

The shepherd gives the sheep food and water once a day and makes sure the sheep have salt to lick. Salt has minerals the sheep need to stay healthy. As spring nears, the shepherd gives the ewes grain, too. Eating grain makes them strong and healthy for giving birth. This is known as lambing time.

Spring lambing is the busiest time. Shepherds watch the ewes carefully to see when they're ready to have their lambs. Sometimes the ewes need help. If a ewe is having trouble giving birth, the shep-herds know how to help the lamb be born.

This lamb stays close to its mother.

After the lambs are born, a shepherd puts each one in a small lambing pen with its mother. Ewes know their lambs only by smell at first. If a new-born lamb strays more than 10 feet (3 meters) from its mother, it's lost. In the lambing pens, the ewes and lambs get to know each other. Now the lambs won't lose their mother when they are among the rest of the flock.

One or two weeks after the lambs are born, most of the male lambs have a simple operation so they don't grow into rams. Afterward they are called wethers. The wethers are raised only for meat.

A farmer bobs, or cuts short, a lamb's tail.

At the same time, the lambs get their tails docked, or shortened. Lambs are born with long tails. If they're not cut short, they may get dirty or diseased.

These ewes feed apart from the lambs.

The lambs start to eat hay when they're two weeks old. The shepherd puts their food in a creep. This is a pen with small openings that lambs can get through, but not ewes. That way, the lambs don't

This man is shearing a sheep.

compete with the ewes for food. They can play with each other in the creep, too.

Soon it's time to shear the grown sheep. A shearer uses a tool similar to an electric razor to cut off the thick wool fleece in one large piece. The shepherd sells it to wool merchants.

Wool sweaters keep us warm.

Wool clothing keeps you warm and dry. Even if a wool sweater gets wet, it will still keep you warm. Wool is flame resistant, so it's safer to wear than other fabrics, such as cotton. And wool clothing lasts a long time.

A shepherd trims a ram's hoof.

There are other things to do in the spring. The sheep need to be dipped in a solution that kills fleas and ticks. Their hooves need to be trimmed, too. If they grow too long, it's hard for the sheep to walk.

When the days get warm, the flock is let out to pasture again. The lambs frisk and play and eat. In the fall, the wethers are big enough to sell for meat. People all around the world enjoy lamb meat.

Finally, it's fall mating time. The whole cycle begins again.

A merchant dyes wool for carpets.

In a marketplace, dyed wool hangs to dry.

Wonderful Wool

People use wool for more than clothing. It makes warm blankets and tough, comfortable rugs and carpets. It is woven into cloth for drapes, upholstery, and cushions. Look around your house. How many different things can you find that are made of wool?

To Find Out More

Here are some additional resources to help you learn more about sheep.

Books

Brady, Peter. **Sheep.** Bridgestone Books, 1996.

Jeunesse, Gallimard. **Farm Animals.** Scholastic, 1998.

Kalman, Bobbie. **Hooray for Sheep Farming!** Crabtree Publishing, 1997.

McGinty, Alice B. **Sheepherding Dogs: Rounding Up the Herd.** Powerkids Press, 1999.

Radtke, Becky. **Farm Activity Book.** Dover Publications, 1997.

Webster, Charlie. **Farm Animals.** Barron's, 1997.

Organizations and Online Sites

CyberSpace Farms
http://www.cyberspaceag. com/tinagreeting.html

Here you can visit a CyberSpace Farm and find out more about farm animals in Creature Features.

Information Dirt Road
http://www.ics.icu.edu/~ pazzani/4H/InfoDirt.html

This site has information about raising farm animals, including sheep.

Kids Farm
http://www.kidsfarm.com

Kids Farm is a lot of fun and educational, too. It is created by people who run a farm in the Colorado Rocky Mountains. It brings you real sights and sounds of animals on the farm.

KidsKorner
http://www.mda.state.mi.us /kids/main.html

The Michigan Department of Agriculture brings children a virtual county fair with the chance to play games, as well as to learn more about farm animals, including sheep.

National 4-H Council
http://www.fourhcouncil. edu

This site will tell you about animal clubs and special interest activities for youth across the United States.

Important Words

creep a feeding pen only lambs can get into

draft a flow of cold air

fleece a sheep's thick wool

lambing pen a small pen where a ewe and its newborn lambs can get to know each other

ornery stubborn and mean

pasture grazing land for animals

predator an animal that hunts another animal for food

teats the nipples on a ewe's udder to nurse its lambs

wether a male lamb raised for meat

Index

Meet the Author

Sara Swan Miller has enjoyed working with children all her life, first as a nursery-school teacher, and later as an outdoor environmental educator at the Mohonk Preserve in New Paltz, New York. Now Ms. Miller is a full-time writer. She has written more than thirty books for children, including *Chickens*, *Cows*, *Goats*, and *Pigs*, in the True Books series.

Photographs ©: BBC Natural History Unit: 2 (Jeff Foott), 21 (Brian Lightfoot), 9 (Magnus Nyman); Ben Klaffke: 7 top, 11 inset bottom, 20, 23, 24, 32, 38, 40; Dembinsky Photo Assoc.: 27 (Rolf Kopfle), 29 (Gijsbert van Frankenhuyzen); Envision: 7 bottom (Steven Needham); Liaison Agency, Inc.: 18 (Wolfgang Kaehler); Peter Arnold Inc.: 15 (John Cancalosi), 26 (Robert C. Gildart), 39 (Gerhard Gscheidle), 14 (S. J. Krasemann), cover (Lior Rubin); Photo Researchers: 43 right (Andy Bernhaut), 16 (Gregory G. Dimijian), 43 left (Stephanie Dinkins), 12 (Michael P. Gadomski), 4 (Rafael Macia), 11 inset top (Stephen Saks); Tony Stone Images: 35 (Christopher Arneson), 42 (Peter Cade), 30 (Anthony Cassidy), 8 (Gerard Del Vecchio), 10, 11 (Robert Frerck), 41; Visuals Unlimited: 37 (Joe McDonald), 1 (William J. Weber).